Along the Lighted Path

THOMAS KINKADE

HARVEST HOUSE PUBLISHERS
EUGENE, OREGON 97402

Along the Lighted Path

Text Copyright © 2002
by Thomas Kinkade, Media Arts Group, Inc., Morgan Hill, CA 95037
and Harvest House Publishers, Eugene OR 97402

Published by Harvest House Publishers
Eugene, OR 97402

ISBN 0-7369-0632-0

Media Arts Group, Inc.
900 Lightpost Way
Morgan Hill, CA 95037
1.800.366.3733

Verses are taken from: the Holy Bible, New International Version®. Copyright © 1973,
1978, 1984 by the International Bible Society. Used by permission of Zondervan Publishing
House; and the King James Version of the Bible.

Design and production by Koechel Peterson & Associates,
Minneapolis, Minnesota

Printed in Hong Kong

02 03 04 05 06 07 08 09 10 11/ NG / 10 9 8 7 6 5 4 3 2 1

*L*ight is the symbol of truth.

— JAMES RUSSELL LOWELL —

The thick sunlight was lavish on the bright water, on the rim of gold-green balsam boughs, the silver birches and tropic ferns, and across the lake it burned on the sturdy shoulders of the mountains.
Over everything was a holy peace.

— LEWIS SINCLAIR—

I am the light of the world.
Whoever follows me will never walk in darkness, but will have the light of life.

— JESUS —

The best remedy for those who are afraid, lonely or unhappy is to go outside, somewhere where they can be quiet, alone with the heavens, nature and God. Because only then does one feel that all is as it should be and that God wishes to see people happy, amidst the simple beauty of nature. As long as this exists, and it certainly always will, I know that then there will always be comfort for every sorrow, whatever the circumstances may be. And I firmly believe that nature brings solace in all troubles.

— ANNE FRANK —

The LORD is my light and my salvation—whom shall I fear? The LORD is the stronghold of my life—of whom shall I be afraid?

— THE BOOK OF PSALMS —

Just think of the illimitable abundance and the marvelous loveliness of light, or of the beauty of the sun and moon and stars.

— SAINT AUGUSTINE —

Begin today! No matter how feeble the light, let it shine as best it may. The world may need just that quality of light which you have.

HENRY C. BLINN

I never trod a rock so bare,
Unblessed by verdure-brightened sod,
But some small flower, half-hidden there,
Exhaled the fragrant breath of God.

— ANONYMOUS —

Just being happy helps other souls along;
Their burdens may be heavy and they not strong;
And your own sky will lighten, if other skies you brighten,
By just being happy with a heart full of song.

— RIPLEY D. SAUNDERS —

9

*I*f the light is…

It is because God said, "Let there be light."

— DANTE GABRIEL ROSSETTI —

Seas roll to waft me,

suns to light me rise;

My footstool earth,

my canopy the skies.

ALEXANDER POPE

Joy is a light that fills you with hope and faith and love.

— ADELA ROGERS ST. JOHNS —

At first a small line of inconceivable splendour emerged on the horizon, which, quickly expanding, the sun appeared in all of his glory, unveiling the whole face of nature, vivifying every colour of the landscape, and sprinkling the dewy earth with glittering light.

— ANN RADCLIFFE —

When one tugs at a single thing in nature, he finds it attached to the rest of the world.

JOHN MUIR

Thomas
Kinkade

Climb the mountains and get their good tidings. Nature's peace will flow into you as sunshine flows into trees. The winds will blow their freshness into you, and the storms their energy, while cares will drop off like falling leaves.

— JOHN MUIR —

My father considered a walk among the mountains as the equivalent of churchgoing.

ALDOUS HUXLEY

*A*bove the elms, all the stars in their turn, beneath the mild airs of summers, in the cold crisp frosts of winter, I watched them above the elms, shining in the sky. They brought to me the thought of greatness of soul. Alone with my thought beneath the stars I prayed in the night. The hours illuminated by the stars were full of beauty and of deep soul prayer.

— RICHARD JEFFERIES —

The path of the righteous is like the first gleam of dawn, shining ever brighter till the full light of day.

THE BOOK OF PROVERBS

Courage, brother! do not stumble,

Though thy path be dark as night;

There's a star to guide the humble,

Trust in God and do the right.

— NORMAN MACLEOD —

How lovely the little river is, with its dark changing
wavelets! It seems to me like a living companion while
I wander along the bank, and listen to its low, placid
voice, as to the voice of one who is deaf and loving.
I remember those large dipping willows. I remember
the stone bridge.

— GEORGE ELIOT —

This fair tree that shadows us from the sun hath grown many years in its place without more unhappiness than the loss of its leaves in winter, which the succeeding season doth generously repair, and shall we be less contented in the place where God has planted us? Or shall there go less time to the making of a man than to the growth of a tree? This stream floweth dimpling and laughing down to the great sea which it knoweth not, yet it doth not fret because the future is hidden; and it were doubtless wise in us to accept the mysteries of life as cheerfully and go forward with a merry heart, considering that we know enough to make us happy and keep us honest for today. A man should be well content if he can see so far ahead of him as the next bend in the stream. What lies beyond let him trust in the hand of God.

— HENRY VAN DYKE —

Strait is the gate, and narrow is the way.

— THE BOOK OF MATTHEW —

But when the sun in all his state

    Illumed the eastern skies,

She passed through Glory's morning-gate,

    And walked in Paradise.

— JAMES ALDRICH —

The sun is a-wait at

the ponderous gate

of the West.

SIDNEY LANIER

20

Under the yaller pines I house,
  When sunshine makes 'em all sweet-scented,
An' hear among their furry boughs
  The baskin' west-wind purr contented.

JAMES RUSSELL LOWELL

No need of the sunlight in heaven we're told,

    The Light of the world is Jesus;

The Lamb is the Light in the city of gold,

    The Light of the world is Jesus.

Come to the Light, 'tis shining for thee;

    Sweetly the Light has dawned upon me,

Once I was blind, but now I can see:

    The Light of the world is Jesus.

— PHILIP P. BLISS —

Afoot and light-hearted, I take to the open road,

Healthy, free, the world before me,

The long brown path before me, leading wherever I choose.

Henceforth I ask not good-fortune—I myself am good fortune;

Henceforth I whimper no more, postpone no more, need nothing,

Strong and content, I travel the open road.

— WALT WHITMAN, "SONG OF THE OPEN ROAD" —

Overhead was a gray expanse of cloud, slightly
stirred, however, by a breeze; so that a gleam of
flickering sunshine might now and then be seen at
its solitary play along the path. This flitting
cheerfulness was always at the farther extremity of
some long vista through the forest.

— NATHANIEL HAWTHORNE —

From thee, great God, we spring, to thee we tend,—
Path, motive, guide, original, and end.

— SAMUEL JOHNSON —

Lord of all being, throned afar,

Thy glory flames from sun and star;

Centre and soul of every sphere,

Yet to each loving heart how near!

Sun of our life, thy quickening ray

Sheds on our path the glow of day:

Star of our hope, thy softened light

Cheers the long watches of the night.

Our midnight is thy smile withdrawn;

Our noontide is thy gracious dawn;

Our rainbow arch, thy mercy's sign:

All, save the clouds of sin, are thine.

Lord of all life, below, above,

Whose light is truth, whose warmth is love;

Before thy ever blazing throne

We ask no lustre of our own.

Grant us thy truth to make us free,

And kindling hearts that burn for thee,

Till all thy living altars claim

One holy light, one heavenly flame.

— OLIVER WENDELL HOLMES
"A SUN-DAY HYMN" —

The path of faith and its difficulties, is that in which we walk with God, and in which we celebrate the triumph which His presence secures to us.

— JOHN DARBY —

Thou wilt show me the path of life:

In thy presence is fullness of joy;

At thy right hand are pleasures for evermore.

— THE BOOK OF PSALMS —

Thy word is a lamp unto my feet,
and a light unto my path.

— THE BOOK OF PSALMS —

Give light, and
the darkness will
disappear of itself.

ERASMUS

For the wonder of each hour

Of the day and of the night,

Hill and vale, and tree and flower,

Sun and moon, and stars of light;

Christ our God, to Thee we raise

This our hymn of grateful praise.

— FOLLIOTT S. PIERPONT —

Our brightest blazes of
gladness are commonly
kindled by unexpected sparks.

SAMUEL JOHNSON

Light is the first of painters. There is no object so foul that intense light will not make it beautiful.

— RALPH WALDO EMERSON —

There are two kinds of light— the glow that illumines, and the glare that obscures.

JAMES THURBER

All finite things reveal infinitude:

The mountain within its singular bright shade

Like the blue shine on freshly frozen snow,

The after-light upon ice-burdened pines;

Odor of basswood upon a mountain slope,

A scene beloved of bees;

Silence of water above a sunken tree:

The pure serene of memory of one man,—

A ripple widening from a single stone

Winding around the waters of the world.

— THEODORE ROETHKE —

Thomas
Kinkade

Life has loveliness to sell,

Music like a curve of gold,

Scent of pine trees in the rain,

Eyes that love you, arms that hold,

And for your spirit's still delight,

Holy thoughts that star the night.

— SARA TEASDALE —

Let your light shine before men, that they may see your good deeds and praise your Father in heaven.

THE BOOK OF MATTHEW

*L*ong, blue, spiky shadows crept out across the snow-fields, while a rosy glow, at first scarce discernible, gradually deepened and suffused every mountain-top, flushing the glaciers and the harsh crags above them. This was the alpenglow, to me one of the most impressive of all the terrestrial manifestations of God. At the touch of this divine light, the mountains seemed to kindle to a rapt, religious consciousness, and stood hushed and waiting like devout worshipers. Just before the alpenglow began to fade, two crimson clouds came streaming across the summit like wings of flame, rendering the sublime scene yet more impressive; then came darkness and the stars.

— JOHN MUIR —

41

For I will pour water on the thirsty land, and streams on the dry ground; I will pour out my Spirit on your offspring, and my blessing on your descendants. They will spring up like grass in a meadow, like poplar trees by flowing streams.

— THE BOOK OF ISAIAH —

I like to think of hope as a guiding light for the human heart.

— THOMAS KINKADE —

We must build our faith not on fading lights but on the Light that never fails.

OSWALD CHAMBERS

etter to light a candle than curse the darkness.

— CHINESE PROVERB —

In him was life; and the
life was the light of men.
And the light shineth in
darkness; and the darkness
comprehended it not.

THE BOOK OF JOHN

Paintings

Thomas Kinkade